D0461134

-Mapographica-

PEOPLE on EARTH

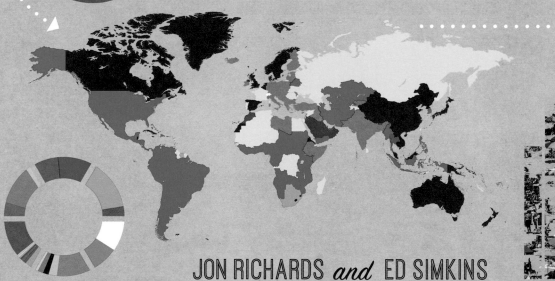

JON RICHARDS *and* ED SIMKINS

Crabtree Publishing Company
www.crabtreebooks.com

Crabtree Publishing Company
www.crabtreebooks.com
1-800-387-7650

Published in Canada
Crabtree Publishing
616 Welland Avenue
St. Catharines, ON
L2M 5V6

Published in the United States
Crabtree Publishing
PMB 59051
350 Fifth Ave, 59th Floor
New York, NY 10118

Published in 2017 by CRABTREE PUBLISHING COMPANY.

First published in 2015 by Wayland
(A division of Hachette Children's Books)
Copyright © Wayland 2015

Authors: Jon Richards, Ed Simkins
Editorial director: Kathy Middleton
Editors: Julia Adams, Jon Richards, and Ellen Rodger
Designer: Ed Simkins
Proofreaders: Wendy Scavuzzo, and Petrice Custance
Prepress technician: Tammy McGarr
Print and production coordinator: Katherine Berti

The publisher would like to thank the following for their kind permission to reproduce their photographs:

Key: (t) top; (c) center; (b) bottom; (l) left; (r) right

Cover, 1br 24-25 and 25t istockphoto.com/rypson, 3a and 30cl NASA, 6-7 istockphoto.com/DRB Images, LLC, 11br istockphoto.com/Carlos_bcn, 12-13 istockphoto.com/spanteldotru, 14-15 istockphoto.com/tomlamela, 18-19 istockphoto.com/ozgurartug, 21t all istockphoto.com/drewhadley, 23t istockphoto.com/Courtney Keating, 24cr istockphoto.com/W6, 24 cl istockphoto.com/dibrova, 24bl istockphoto.com/WillSelarep, 24br istockphoto.com/Nikada, 25bl istockphoto.com/06photo, 27t all istockphoto.com/bluestocking, 28-29 istockphoto.com/Zurijeta, 28cr istockphoto.com/Nikada, 29t istockphoto.com/Yoav Peled, 29tl istockphoto.com/afby71, 29tc istockphoto.com/traveler1116, 29m istockphoto.com/oytun karadayi, 29cr istockphoto.com/Rufous52, 30c istockphoto.com/nicoolay, 30cr istockphoto.com/Manakin

Every attempt has been made to clear copyright. Should there be any inadvertent omission, please apply to the publisher for rectification.

The website addresses (URLs) included in this book were valid at the time of going to press. However, it is possible that contents or addresses may have changed since the publication of this book. No responsibility for any such changes can be accepted by either the author or the Publisher.

Printed in Canada/072016/PB20160525

Library and Archives Canada Cataloguing in Publication

Richards, Jon, 1970-, author
      People on Earth / Jon Richards, Ed Simkins.

(Mapographica: your world in infographics)
Includes index.
Issued in print and electronic formats.
ISBN 978-0-7787-2656-2 (hardback).--
ISBN 978-0-7787-2660-9 (paperback).--
ISBN 978-1-4271-1796-0 (html)

      1. Human beings--Miscellanea--Juvenile literature.
I. Simkins, Ed, author II. Title.

GN31.5.R54 2016   j301   C2016-902665-5
                                        C2016-902666-3

Library of Congress Cataloging-in-Publication Data

Names: Richards, Jon, 1970- author.
Title: People on earth / Jon Richards and Ed Simkins.
Description: New York, New York : Crabtree Publishing, 2017. |
Series: Mapographica: your world in infographics | Includes index.
Identifiers: LCCN 2016016681 (print) | LCCN 2016024756 (ebook) |
ISBN 9780778726562 (reinforced library binding) |
ISBN 9780778726609 (pbk.) |
ISBN 9781427117960 (electronic HTML)
Subjects: LCSH: Human geography--Juvenile literature.
Classification: LCC GF48 .R54 2017 (print) | LCC GF48 (ebook) |
DDC 304.2--dc23
LC record available at https://lccn.loc.gov/2016016681

CONTENTS

— The world in 100 people —

If you reduced the world's population to just 100 people, an average person would live in a town in Asia, speak Chinese, be able to read and write, be between 15 and 64 years old, and would not be undernourished or overweight.

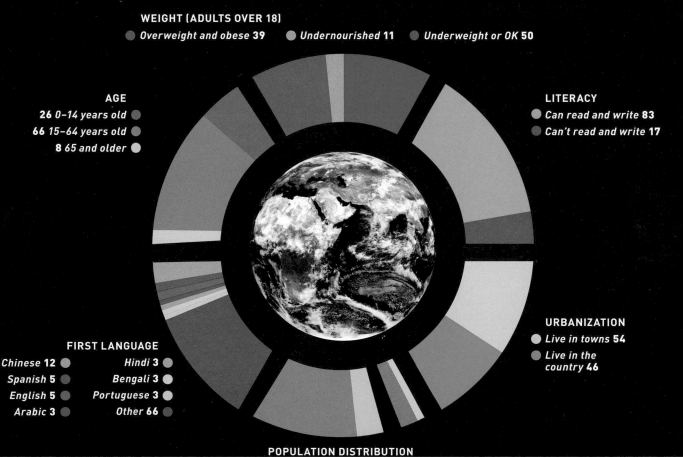

WEIGHT (ADULTS OVER 18)
Overweight and obese **39**   Undernourished **11**   Underweight or OK **50**

AGE
26 0–14 years old
66 15–64 years old
8 65 and older

LITERACY
Can read and write **83**
Can't read and write **17**

FIRST LANGUAGE
Chinese **12**   Hindi **3**
Spanish **5**   Bengali **3**
English **5**   Portuguese **3**
Arabic **3**   Other **66**

URBANIZATION
Live in towns **54**
Live in the country **46**

POPULATION DISTRIBUTION
Asia **60**   Europe **11**   North America **5**
Africa **15**   Latin America and Caribbean **9**

— Human —
WORLD

The world is divided into large landmasses, called continents. The 7 billion people who live on the planet are not scattered evenly across these continents. More than 60 percent of these people live in just one continent—Asia.

EUROPE

NORTH AMERICA

ASIA

AFRICA

SOUTH AMERICA

AUSTRALIA/ OCEANIA

NORTH AMERICA

Number of countries
●●●●●●●●●●●●●●●●●●
●●●●●●●● 26

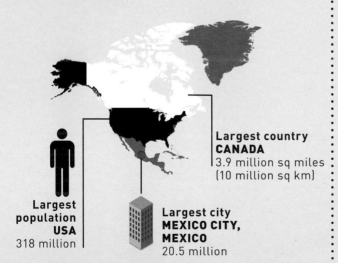

Largest country
CANADA
3.9 million sq miles
(10 million sq km)

Largest population
USA
318 million

Largest city
MEXICO CITY, MEXICO
20.5 million

Total area
9.5 million sq miles
(24.7 million sq km)

Total population
556 million

SOUTH AMERICA

Number of countries
●●●●●●●●●●●●●●●● 16

Largest country
BRAZIL
3.3 million sq miles
(8.5 million sq km)

Largest population
BRAZIL
202.7 million

Largest city
SAO PAULO, BRAZIL
19.9 million

Total area
6.9 million sq miles
(17.8 million sq km)

Total population
401 million

EUROPE

Number of countries
●●●●●●●●●●●●●●●●●●●●
●●●●●●●●●●●●●●●●●●●●
●●●●●●● **47**

Largest population
RUSSIA
(European region)
110 million

Largest country
RUSSIA
(European region)
1.5 million sq miles
(4 million sq km)

Largest city
MOSCOW,
RUSSIA
11.6 million

Total area
3.9 million sq miles
(10.2 million sq km)

Total population
740 million

ASIA

Number of countries
●●●●●●●●●●●●●●●●●●●●
●●●●●●●●●●●●●●●●●●●●
●●●●●●●●●●●● **52**

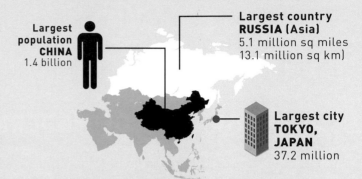

Largest population
CHINA
1.4 billion

Largest country
RUSSIA (Asia)
5.1 million sq miles
13.1 million sq km)

Largest city
TOKYO,
JAPAN
37.2 million

Total area
17.2 million sq miles
(44.6 million sq km)

Total population
4.3 billion

5

AFRICA

Number of countries
●●●●●●●●●●●●●●●●●●●●
●●●●●●●●●●●●●●●●●●●●
●●●●●●●●●●●●●●●●● **57**

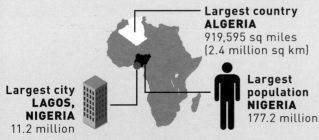

Largest city
LAGOS,
NIGERIA
11.2 million

Largest country
ALGERIA
919,595 sq miles
(2.4 million sq km)

Largest population
NIGERIA
177.2 million

Total area
11.7 million sq miles
(30.2 sq million km)

Total population
1.1 billion

AUSTRALIA/ OCEANIA

Number of countries
●●●●●●●●●●●●●●●●●●●●●●●●●●●● **19**

Largest population
AUSTRALIA
22.5 million

Largest country
AUSTRALIA
3 million sq miles
(77.7 million sq km)

Largest city
SYDNEY,
AUSTRALIA
4.5 million

Total area
3.3 million sq miles
(8.5 million sq km)

Total population
38 million

— Human —
ORIGINS

Modern humans, or *Homo sapiens*, first appeared in Africa about 200,000 years ago. It was another 130,000 to 140,000 years before they started to move out of Africa. By about 50,000 years ago, humans had reached Southeast Asia and Australia.

MIGRATION OF MODERN HUMANS

Driven by the need for food and a place to settle, humans started to migrate out of Africa to other parts of the world.

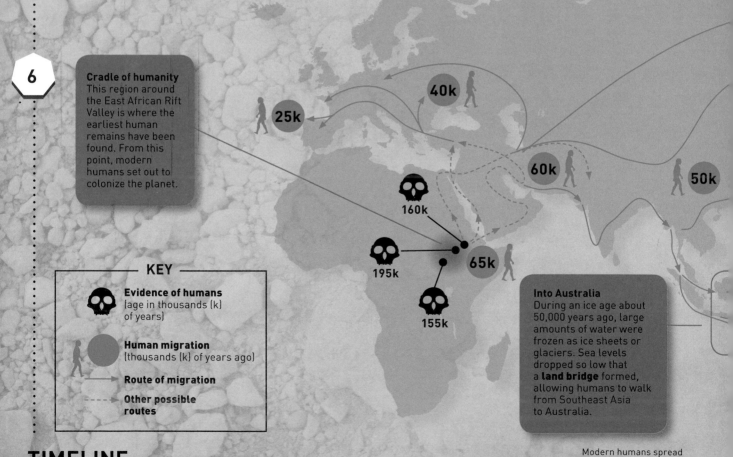

6

Cradle of humanity
This region around the East African Rift Valley is where the earliest human remains have been found. From this point, modern humans set out to colonize the planet.

40k

25k

60k

50k

160k

195k

65k

155k

KEY

🕱 **Evidence of humans**
(age in thousands (k) of years)

🚶 **Human migration**
(thousands (k) of years ago)

— **Route of migration**

- - - **Other possible routes**

Into Australia
During an ice age about 50,000 years ago, large amounts of water were frozen as ice sheets or glaciers. Sea levels dropped so low that a **land bridge** formed, allowing humans to walk from Southeast Asia to Australia.

TIMELINE

80,000 years ago

Modern humans spread across S.E. Asia

Emergence of modern humans in Africa

Ice age begins

Modern humans begin to leave Africa

Population explosion in Africa

200,000 years ago

78,000 years ago

65,000 years ago

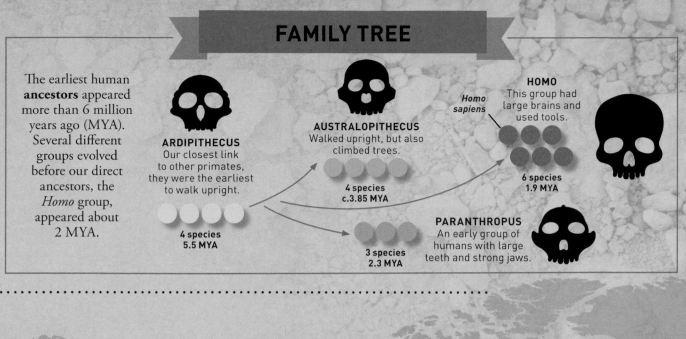

FAMILY TREE

The earliest human **ancestors** appeared more than 6 million years ago (MYA). Several different groups evolved before our direct ancestors, the *Homo* group, appeared about 2 MYA.

ARDIPITHECUS
Our closest link to other primates, they were the earliest to walk upright.

4 species
5.5 MYA

AUSTRALOPITHECUS
Walked upright, but also climbed trees.

4 species
c.3.85 MYA

Homo sapiens

HOMO
This group had large brains and used tools.

6 species
1.9 MYA

PARANTHROPUS
An early group of humans with large teeth and strong jaws.

3 species
2.3 MYA

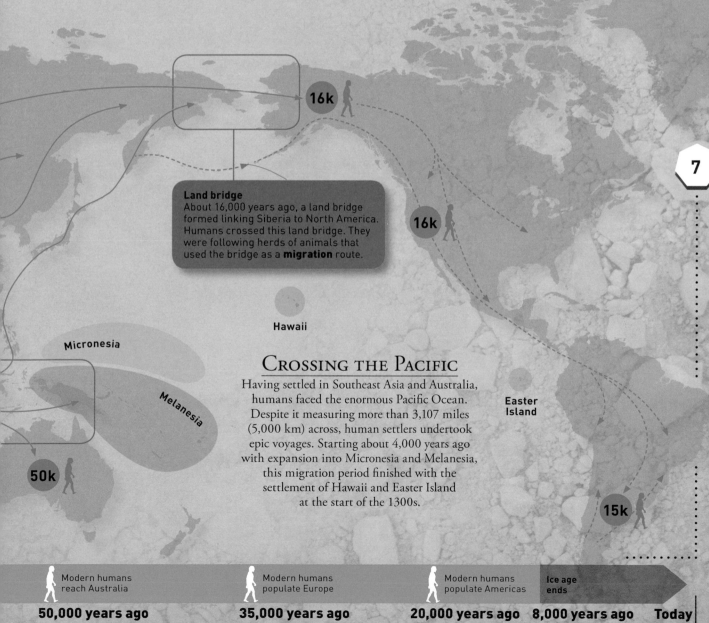

16k

16k

Land bridge
About 16,000 years ago, a land bridge formed linking Siberia to North America. Humans crossed this land bridge. They were following herds of animals that used the bridge as a **migration** route.

Hawaii

Micronesia

Melanesia

Easter Island

CROSSING THE PACIFIC

Having settled in Southeast Asia and Australia, humans faced the enormous Pacific Ocean. Despite it measuring more than 3,107 miles (5,000 km) across, human settlers undertook epic voyages. Starting about 4,000 years ago with expansion into Micronesia and Melanesia, this migration period finished with the settlement of Hawaii and Easter Island at the start of the 1300s.

50k

15k

Modern humans reach Australia	Modern humans populate Europe	Modern humans populate Americas	Ice age ends	
50,000 years ago	**35,000 years ago**	**20,000 years ago**	**8,000 years ago**	**Today**

— Population — GROWTH

How quickly a country grows depends on a number of things, including the availability of healthcare, how many children are born, how long people live, and how wealthy they are. While the populations of some countries and regions are predicted to grow very quickly, others are predicted to shrink!

MOST POPULATED COUNTRIES

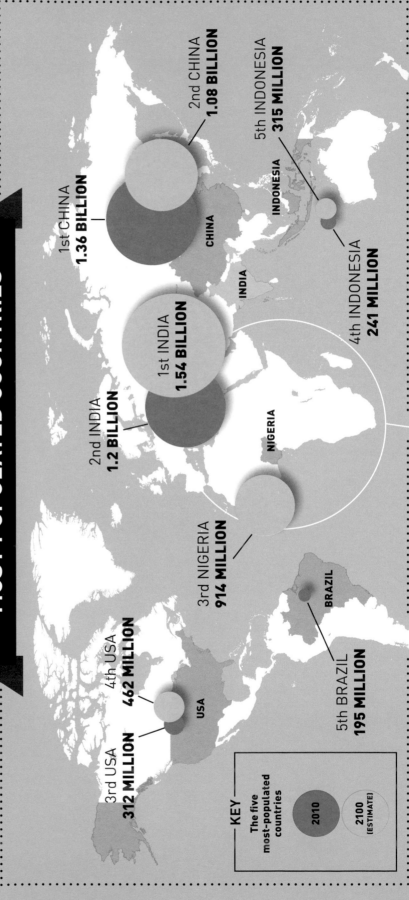

2nd CHINA
1.08 BILLION

1st CHINA
1.36 BILLION

5th INDONESIA
315 MILLION

CHINA

INDONESIA

INDIA

4th INDONESIA
241 MILLION

1st INDIA
1.54 BILLION

2nd INDIA
1.2 BILLION

NIGERIA

3rd NIGERIA
914 MILLION

BRAZIL

5th BRAZIL
195 MILLION

USA

4th USA
462 MILLION

3rd USA
312 MILLION

KEY

The five most-populated countries

2010

2100 (ESTIMATE)

FERTILITY RATES

The average number of children each woman gives birth to in her lifetime is known as the fertility rate. If the fertility rate is high, then it is likely that a country's population is growing quickly. These figures show some of the highest and lowest fertility rates in the world.

Countries with some of the highest fertility rates (children per woman)

NIGER **6.89**   AFGHANISTAN **5.43**

Countries with some of the lowest fertility rates (children per woman)

SINGAPORE **0.80**   SOUTH KOREA **1.25**

10. LIBYA **3.08%**

1. LEBANON **9.37%**

4. JORDAN **3.86%**

5. QATAR **3.58%**

3. SOUTH SUDAN **4.12%**

9. UGANDA **3.24%**

6. MALAWI **3.33%**

2. ZIMBABWE **4.36%**

7. NIGER **3.28%**

8. BURUNDI **3.28%**

This map shows the ten fastest-growing countries and the percentages their populations are growing each year.

BIGGER AND BIGGER

With the fastest-growing countries located in Africa, the population of that continent will soar over the next 100 years. By 2100, it will have nearly quadrupled in size.

Predicted populations of each continent from 2010 to 2100:

POPULATION 2010

EUROPE 740 million
AFRICA 1.1 billion
NORTH AMERICA 556 million
SOUTH AMERICA 401 million
AUSTRALIA & OCEANIA 38 million
ASIA 4.3 billion

POPULATION 2100 (ESTIMATE)

EUROPE 639 million
AFRICA 4.2 billion
NORTH AMERICA 513 million
SOUTH AMERICA 467 million
AUSTRALIA & OCEANIA 47 million
ASIA 4.7 billion

AVERAGE FAMILY

Levels of wealth vary greatly around the world. In general, richer countries grow more slowly than poorer countries. People in poorer countries, such as Burkina Faso in Africa, tend to have larger families than those in richer countries, such as the United States. This increases the number of family members who can earn money, and the older children can care for the old and very young.

Average USA household size **2.6**

Average BURKINA FASO household size **5.9**

A LONG LIFE?

Today, the average **life expectancy** around the world is 70, with men living an average of 68 years and women an average of 73 years. How long you live depends on how wealthy you are, whether you have access to proper **sanitation**, such as a toilet, and the quality of your diet.

AVERAGE AGES

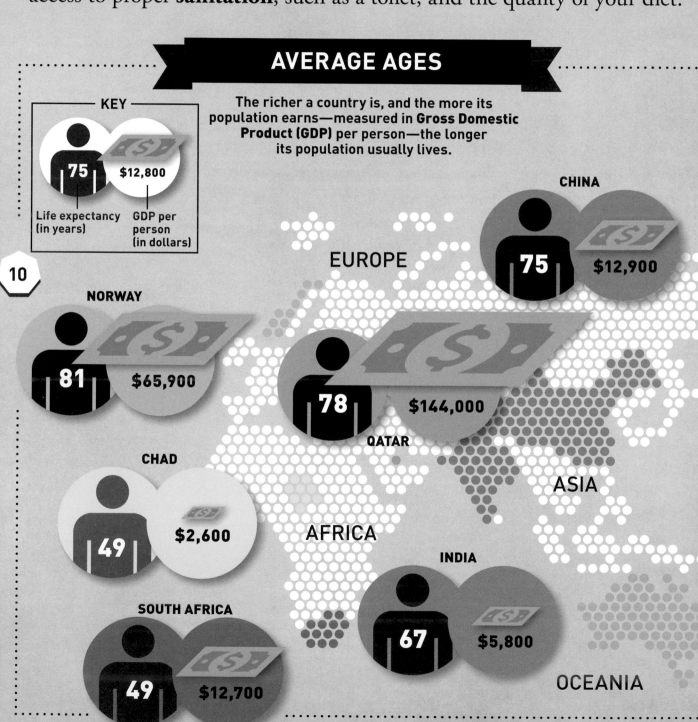

KEY

75 — Life expectancy (in years)

$12,800 — GDP per person (in dollars)

The richer a country is, and the more its population earns—measured in **Gross Domestic Product (GDP)** per person—the longer its population usually lives.

CHINA 75 $12,900

EUROPE

NORWAY 81 $65,900

78 $144,000 **QATAR**

ASIA

CHAD 49 $2,600

AFRICA

INDIA 67 $5,800

SOUTH AFRICA 49 $12,700

OCEANIA

KEEP IT CLEAN

Countries with good sanitation are able to get rid of human waste cleanly and efficiently. This helps to prevent the spread of fatal diseases and increases life expectancy, allowing people to live longer and healthier lives.

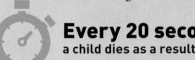 **Every 20 seconds** a child dies as a result of poor sanitation.

Access to sanitation (% of world population)

1990 **49%** 2010 **63%** 2015 **67%**

Access to sanitation (% of country's population)

SOUTH SUDAN **16%**   KENYA **31%**

INDONESIA **71%**   PANAMA **80%**   GERMANY **100%**

The World Bank lists 38 countries whose people have 100% access to improved sanitation facilities. These include the United States, Canada, the United Kingdom, Saudi Arabia, Australia, and South Korea.

NORTH AMERICA

USA
79 $54,800

AUSTRALIA/OCEANIA
82 $46,600

HAITI
63 $1,800

SOUTH AMERICA

AFRICA 59 (male 58, female 60)

ASIA 71 (male 69, female 73)

SOUTH AMERICA 75 (male 71, female 78)

NORTH AMERICA 79 (male 77, female 81)

AUSTRALIA/OCEANIA 77 (male 75, female 79)

EUROPE 78 (male 74, female 81)

Average life expectancy by continent (in years)

Diseases and DOCTORS

Death from disease is a constant threat in any part of the world. The key to fighting disease is a country's health system and the number of doctors and clinics or hospitals people have access to.

MOST LIKELY CAUSES OF DEATH

This world map shows the diseases and conditions that cause the greatest number of deaths in each country.

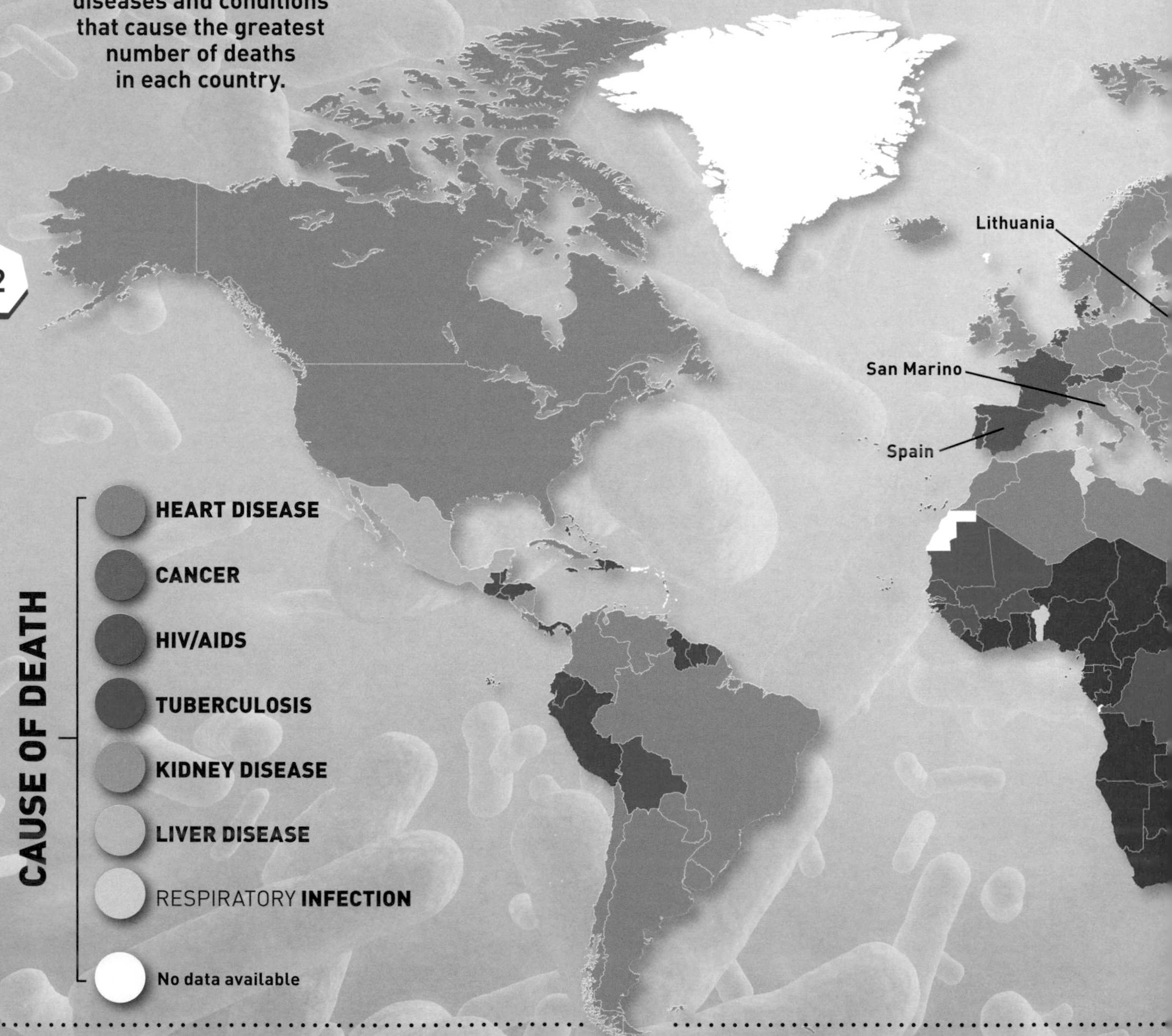

Lithuania

San Marino

Spain

12

CAUSE OF DEATH

- HEART DISEASE
- CANCER
- HIV/AIDS
- TUBERCULOSIS
- KIDNEY DISEASE
- LIVER DISEASE
- RESPIRATORY INFECTION
- No data available

DISEASE AND WEALTH

The wealth of a country has an impact on the diseases to which its people are most susceptible. People living in poorer countries are more likely to die from infectious diseases, because their countries have fewer doctors, hospitals, and clinics. People in richer countries are more likely to die from conditions caused by bad habits, such as smoking.

Lower respiratory infections
91

Diarrheal diseases
53

Top 3 causes of death in low-income countries
(deaths per 100,000 people)

HIV/AIDS
65

Top 3 causes of death in high-income countries
(deaths per 100,000 people)

Stroke
95

Trachea, bronchus, lung cancers
49

Heart disease
158

DOCTORS

Countries with a high number of doctors are likely to have good **health care**, which aids in preventing and controling diseases. According to the World Health Organization, fewer than 2.3 health workers (doctors, nurses, and midwives) per 1,000 people is not enough to meet healthcare needs.

Doctors per 1,000 people

Georgia

Bhutan

Laos

Qatar

Cambodia

Indonesia

Mozambique

— LOWEST —

Mozambique 0.1
Laos 0.2
Indonesia 0.2
Cambodia 0.2
Bhutan 0.3

— HIGHEST —

Qatar 7.7
San Marino 5.1
Georgia 4.2
Lithuania 4.1
Spain 3.7

Living in
CITIES

Since the earliest cities were founded more than 10,000 years ago, more and more people have been moving to urban settlements. This movement of people from the country to cities is called **urbanization**.

PEOPLE LIVING IN URBAN AREAS
AND CITIES WITH MORE THAN 10 MILLION PEOPLE

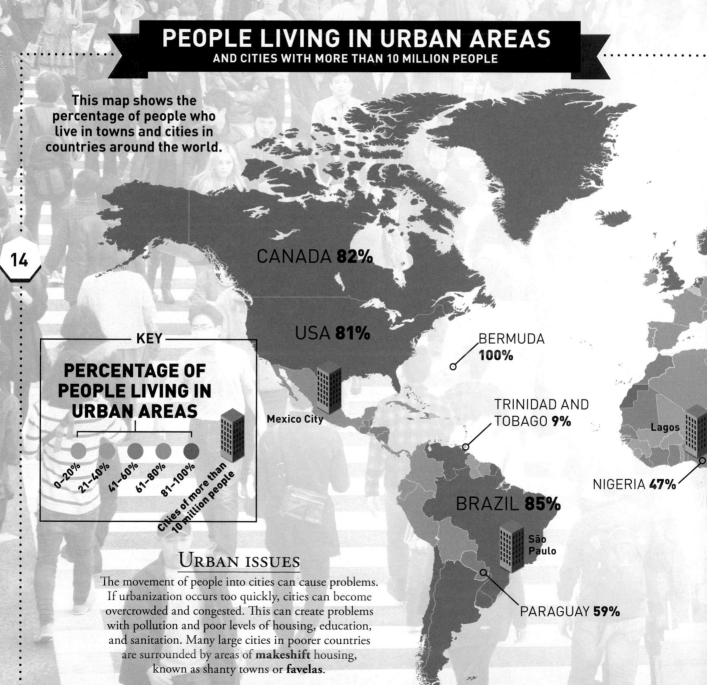

This map shows the percentage of people who live in towns and cities in countries around the world.

KEY

PERCENTAGE OF PEOPLE LIVING IN URBAN AREAS

0–20% 21–40% 41–60% 61–80% 81–100%

Cities of more than 10 million people

CANADA **82%**

USA **81%**

Mexico City

BERMUDA **100%**

TRINIDAD AND TOBAGO **9%**

Lagos

NIGERIA **47%**

BRAZIL **85%**

São Paulo

PARAGUAY **59%**

URBAN ISSUES

The movement of people into cities can cause problems. If urbanization occurs too quickly, cities can become overcrowded and congested. This can create problems with pollution and poor levels of housing, education, and sanitation. Many large cities in poorer countries are surrounded by areas of **makeshift** housing, known as shanty towns or **favelas**.

CHANGES IN LEVELS OF URBANIZATION (%)

	WORLD	AFRICA	ASIA	EUROPE	LATIN AMERICA AND CARIBBEAN	NORTH AMERICA	AUSTRALIA & OCEANIA
1950	29.6	14.0	17.5	51.1	41.3	63.9	62.4
2000	46.6	34.5	37.5	70.9	75.3	79.1	70.5
2050	66.4	55.9	64.2	82.0	86.2	87.4	73.5

RUSSIAN FEDERATION 74%

Moscow

Istanbul

Cairo

Karachi

Lahore

Mumbai

Dhaka

Beijing

Tianjin

Seoul

Tokyo

Shanghai

Shenzhen

Guangzhou

JAPAN 92%

32% INDIA

EGYPT 43%

SINGAPORE 100%

INDONESIA 52%

AUSTRALIA & OCEANIA 89%

TONGA 24%

SUB-SAHARAN AFRICA

71.8% of city dwellers live in slums.

30–50% lack access to clean water.

Child mortality is 2.5 times greater in slums than other areas.

Currently, **1 billion people** live in slums.

This will double to 2 billion in the next 30 years.

Types of GOVERNMENT

Governments differ throughout the world, and so does the ability of citizens to have a say in the way they are governed. In democracies, people can vote for their leaders, while in absolute **monarchies** or one-party states, people cannot choose who governs them.

THE WORLD'S GOVERNMENTS

This map shows the different types of government used by countries around the world.

Switzerland
This Alpine country has a federal system made up of 26 regions called Cantons. It has no full-time president, and presidential duties are carried out by one of the government's department heads.

— KEY —

Types of Governments

- Republics
- Constitutional monarchies
- Absolute monarchies
- Single political party or coalition
- Other government systems

Ruling parties
Republics make up nearly 75 percent of the types of government around the world.

Number of countries per type of government

| 146 | 38 | 6 | 7 | 1 |

LONGEST RULE

Paul Biya of Cameroon holds the record for the longest ruling non-royal national leader.
He came to power on June 30, 1975, and in his time as president he has seen seven United States presidents come and go.

Map labels: Greenland, Canada, United States, Cuba, United Kingdom, Spain, Cameroon

Number of monarchs worldwide

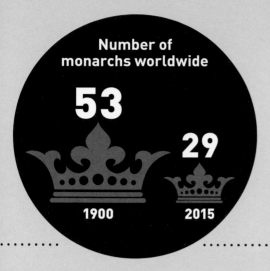

53 1900

29 2015

Longest-reigning monarchs

Sobhuza II
Swaziland
December 1899 – August 1982
82 years, 254 days
①

Bernhard VII Lippe
Holy Roman Empire
August 1429 – April 1511
81 years, 234 days
②

William IV Henneberg-Schleusingen
Holy Roman Empire
May 1480 – January 1559
78 years, 243 days
③

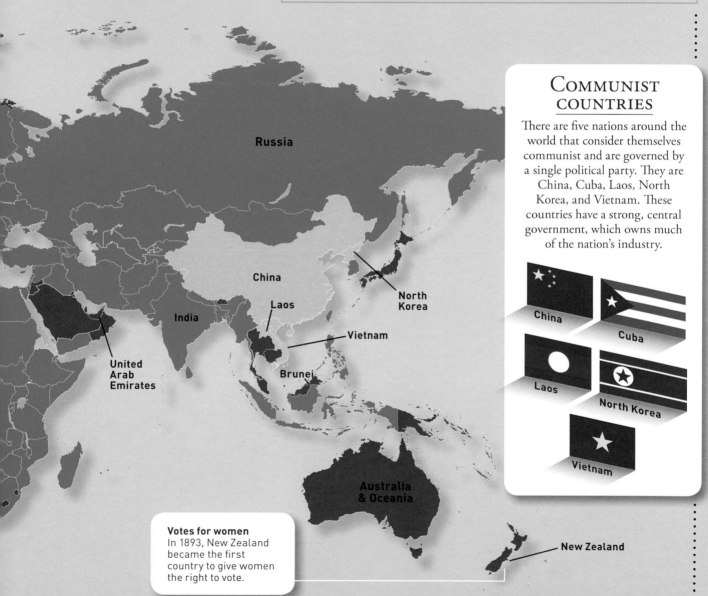

Russia

China

India

Laos

North Korea

Vietnam

Brunei

United Arab Emirates

Australia & Oceania

New Zealand

COMMUNIST COUNTRIES

There are five nations around the world that consider themselves communist and are governed by a single political party. They are China, Cuba, Laos, North Korea, and Vietnam. These countries have a strong, central government, which owns much of the nation's industry.

China

Cuba

Laos

North Korea

Vietnam

Votes for women
In 1893, New Zealand became the first country to give women the right to vote.

Armed FORCES

The size of a country's armed forces depends on how involved it is in conflicts around the world, as well as its relations with its neighbors. South Korea may be small, but tension with North Korea requires the country to maintain a large army.

GLOBAL ARMED FORCES

This map shows the countries that have the biggest armed forces and those that spend the most on arms each year. It also shows the numbers of personnel (active and reserve), tanks, aircraft, and ships.

RUSSIA
3.3 million
15,398
352
3,429

INDIA
3.5 million
6,464
202
1,905

JAPAN
PERSONNEL 305,000
TANKS 678
AIRCRAFT 1,613
SHIPS 131

TURKEY
PERSONNEL 596,000
TANKS 3,778
AIRCRAFT 1,020
SHIPS 115

UNITED KINGDOM
PERSONNEL 329,000
TANKS 407
AIRCRAFT 936
SHIPS 66

FRANCE
PERSONNEL 398,531
TANKS 423
AIRCRAFT 1,264
SHIPS 113

SOUTH KOREA

2,381
1,412
3.5 million
166

CHINA

9,150
2,860
4.6 million
673

USA

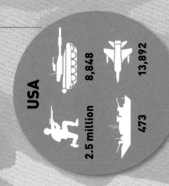

8,848
13,892
2.5 million
473

GERMANY
PERSONNEL 328,000
TANKS 408
AIRCRAFT 710
SHIPS 82

NUCLEAR POWERS

There are nine countries that have nuclear warheads.
While many of these are in storage or waiting to be dismantled,
the United States and Russia have about 1,800 that are on
constant high-alert status and can be fired at a moment's notice.

= 100 WARHEADS

INDIA 90–110 (0.5%)

ISRAEL 80 (0.4%)

NORTH KOREA FEWER THAN 10 (0.06%)

FRANCE 300 (1.8%)

CHINA 250 (1.5%)

UK 225 (1.3%)

PAKISTAN 100–120 (0.6%)

USA 7,315 (44%)

RUSSIA 8,000 (48% OF GLOBAL NUMBER)

TOTAL: ABOUT **16,400**

— Getting — HEAVY

Obesity is a problem in many parts of the world, with more than one third of the people in some countries being extremely overweight. This is often the result of bad habits, such as eating too much and eating foods that are high in calories.

LEVELS OF OBESITY

This map shows the percentages of household income spent on food in different countries around the world, and the levels of obesity. In general, wealthier countries spend a smaller percentage on food, but have higher levels of obesity.

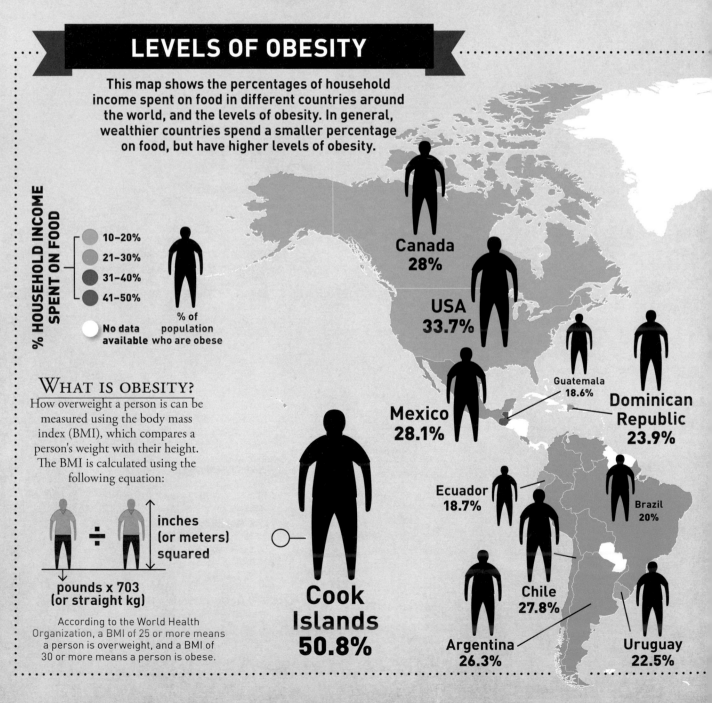

% HOUSEHOLD INCOME SPENT ON FOOD

- 10–20%
- 21–30%
- 31–40%
- 41–50%
- No data available

% of population who are obese

WHAT IS OBESITY?
How overweight a person is can be measured using the body mass index (BMI), which compares a person's weight with their height. The BMI is calculated using the following equation:

inches (or meters) squared

÷

pounds x 703 (or straight kg)

According to the World Health Organization, a BMI of 25 or more means a person is overweight, and a BMI of 30 or more means a person is obese.

Canada
28%

USA
33.7%

Mexico
28.1%

Guatemala
18.6%

Dominican Republic
23.9%

Cook Islands
50.8%

Ecuador
18.7%

Brazil
20%

Chile
27.8%

Argentina
26.3%

Uruguay
22.5%

OBESITY AND CALORIES

How much you should eat depends on your age, metabolism, and how active you are. Generally, adult men should eat 2,500 calories a day on average, and women should eat about 2,000 calories a day.

% of population who are obese

Average calories eaten per day

India 2,300
3.2%

USA 3,770
32.6%

U.K. 3,440
26.9%

Argentina 3,000
23.6%

Democratic Republic of the Congo
1,590 1.9%

These figures show the number of **calories people eat** in each country, and the **percentage of obese people** living there.

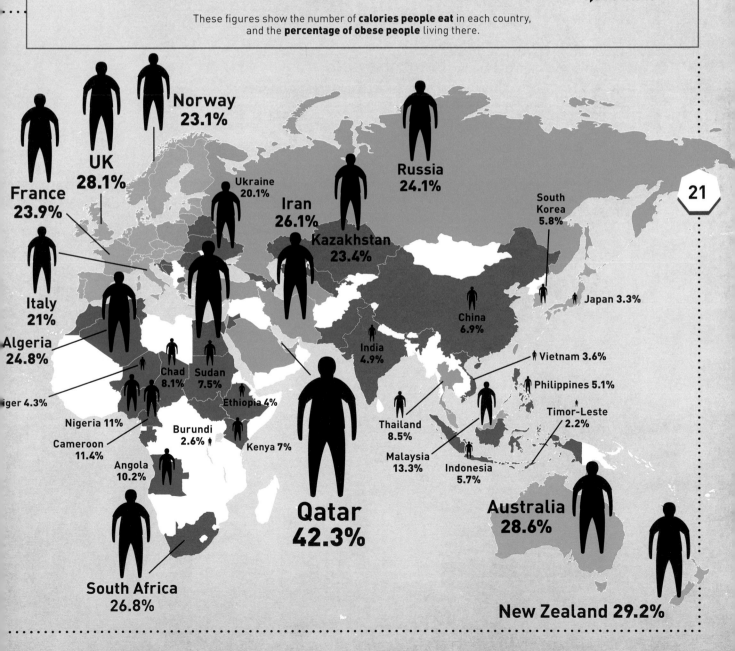

Norway
23.1%

UK
28.1%

France
23.9%

Italy
21%

Algeria
24.8%

Niger 4.3%

Nigeria 11%

Cameroon
11.4%

Angola
10.2%

South Africa
26.8%

Chad
8.1%

Sudan
7.5%

Ethiopia 4%

Burundi
2.6%

Kenya 7%

Ukraine
20.1%

Iran
26.1%

Kazakhstan
23.4%

Russia
24.1%

Qatar
42.3%

India
4.9%

China
6.9%

South Korea
5.8%

Japan 3.3%

Vietnam 3.6%

Philippines 5.1%

Thailand
8.5%

Malaysia
13.3%

Indonesia
5.7%

Timor-Leste
2.2%

Australia
28.6%

New Zealand 29.2%

21

—Global—
LANGUAGES

There are more than 7,000 languages spoken around the world. Some of the most popular, such as Mandarin and Hindi, are spoken in countries with huge populations. Others, including English and Spanish, are widely spoken because of the colonial history of their original countries.

MAJOR LANGUAGES

Some countries have several different languages, or two official languages, such as in Canada. This map represents the most widely used language in each country.

LANGUAGE
- Arabic
- Bengali
- English
- German
- French
- Hindi
- Mandarin Chinese
- Portuguese
- Russian
- Spanish
- Other, such as Italian, Greek, Urdu, Swedish, Arabic, or Indonesian

WRITING SYSTEMS
Written languages use a system of symbols to represent various letters, groups of letters, sounds, or even entire words. These symbols range from simple lines and shapes to complex illustrations.

Latin alphabet

Latin (used in many European languages)

Ελληνικο αλφαβητο

Greek (used in Greek)

LANGUAGES OF THE INTERNET

The large number of Internet users in North America, the United Kingdom, and Australia means that English is by far the most common language used to search the Internet.

Languages of Internet users (millions of users)

Language	Users
ENGLISH	800.6
CHINESE	649.4
SPANISH	222.4
ARABIC	135.6
PORTUGUESE	121.8
JAPANESE	109.6

RUSSIAN **87.5**
GERMAN **81.1**
FRENCH **78.9**
MALAYSIAN **75.5**

MOST POPULAR LANGUAGES

At one point in history, the British Empire covered almost one third of the globe. This is why English is now spoken in more countries than any other language. Portugal, France, and Spain also had empires, and their languages are spoken around the world, while Arabic dominates nations in northern Africa and the Middle East.

23

Portuguese **11**

French **51**

Russian **11**

English 101 countries

Arabic **59**

Spanish **31**

Кириллица алфавит
Cyrillic (used in Russian)

日本語の漢字
Kanji (used in Japanese)

Vacation TIME

Key factors that affect how much time people spend on vacation and where they go include cost, the amount of vacation they can have, and what their own country has to offer in terms of facilities and climate.

MOST POPULAR DESTINATIONS

These figures show how many foreign tourists visit each of these countries every year, and the most popular tourist attractions.

Most visited attraction
Notre Dame Cathedral, Paris

FRANCE 84.7 million **1**

USA 69.8 million **2**

Most visited attraction
Times Square, New York City

SPAIN 60.7 million **3**

ITALY 47.7 million **5**

Most visited attraction
Alhambra Palace, Granada

Most visited attraction
St. Peter's Basilica, Vatican City

TAKING TIME OFF

These figures show the countries that guarantee their workers the highest and lowest amount of paid vacation.

Countries with the most time off (in days)

38	AUSTRIA
35	PORTUGAL
34	SPAIN, GERMANY
31	ITALY, FRANCE
30	BELGIUM, NEW ZEALAND
28	AUSTRALIA
25	BRAZIL
19	CANADA

Countries with the least time off (in days)

10	JAPAN
5	CHINA
0	UNITED STATES*

*Of all wealthy nations, the United States is the only one that does not require employers to offer employees paid vacation time.

CHINA 55.7 million

4

Most visited attraction
Forbidden City, Beijing

TOURIST MONEY

Tourists and vacationers can bring a lot of money into a country. These figures show which countries earn the most from tourism.

Earnings from tourism
(billions of dollars per year)

ITALY $41.2

CHINA $50

FRANCE $53.6

SPAIN $55.9

USA $126.2

Education—
AND LITERACY

The ability to read and write is the basis of a good education, but **literacy** levels vary around the world, largely depending on a nation's wealth. Education levels can also vary between men and women, even in the same country.

LITERACY RATES

This map shows the average percentages of people who can read and write in countries with some of the highest and lowest literacy rates in the world, as well as the percentages of men and women who are literate.

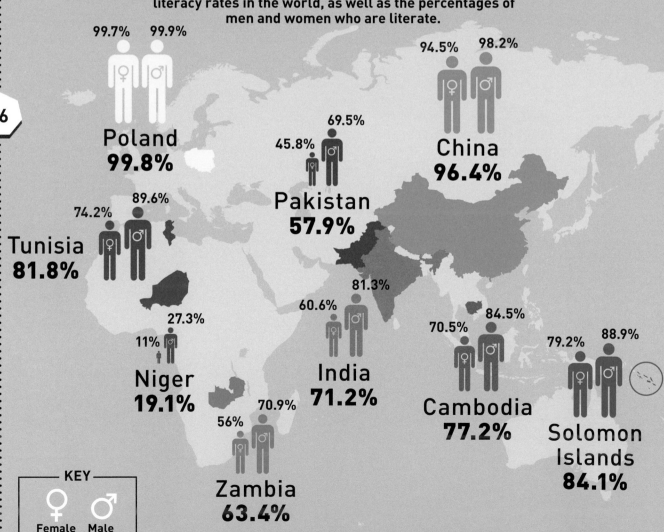

Poland
99.7% 99.9%
99.8%

Tunisia
74.2% 89.6%
81.8%

Niger
11% 27.3%
19.1%

Pakistan
45.8% 69.5%
57.9%

India
60.6% 81.3%
71.2%

Zambia
56% 70.9%
63.4%

China
94.5% 98.2%
96.4%

Cambodia
70.5% 84.5%
77.2%

Solomon Islands
79.2% 88.9%
84.1%

KEY
♀ Female   ♂ Male

YEARS SPENT IN EDUCATION

Wealthier countries, such as Australia, usually spend more money on their schools, universities, and colleges than poorer countries such as Niger, in Africa. As such, people in wealthier countries will spend longer in school, gaining a higher literacy rate and more qualifications.

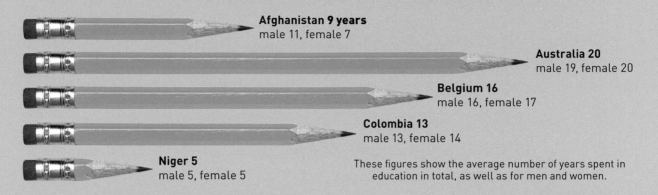

Afghanistan 9 years
male 11, female 7

Australia 20
male 19, female 20

Belgium 16
male 16, female 17

Colombia 13
male 13, female 14

Niger 5
male 5, female 5

These figures show the average number of years spent in education in total, as well as for men and women.

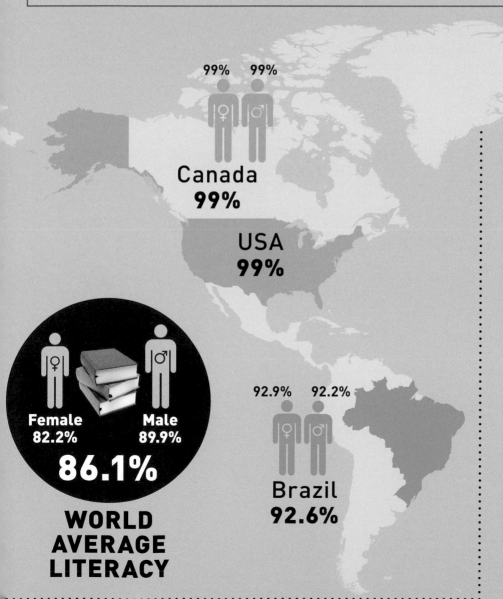

99% 99%

Canada
99%

USA
99%

92.9% 92.2%

Brazil
92.6%

Female 82.2% **Male 89.9%**
86.1%
WORLD AVERAGE LITERACY

BEYOND SCHOOL

Higher education at a college or university allows a person to study for a degree or other similar qualification. People living in wealthier countries are more likely to go to college or university.

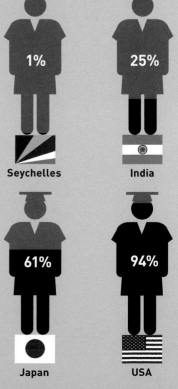

Percentage of population going on to higher education

1%
Seychelles

25%
India

61%
Japan

94%
USA

RELIGION

More than 80 percent of the world's population, or 5.8 billion people, are members of a religion. Of these 5.8 billion, 2.2 billion are Christian, 1.6 billion are Muslim, 1 billion are Hindu, 500 million are Buddhist, and 14 million are Jewish.

MAJOR RELIGIONS

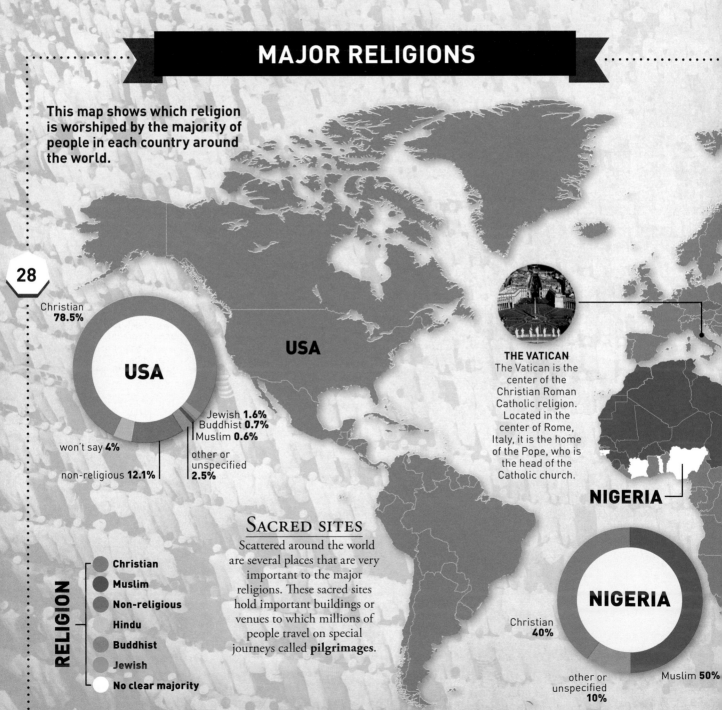

This map shows which religion is worshiped by the majority of people in each country around the world.

USA

Christian **78.5%**

USA

Jewish **1.6%**
Buddhist **0.7%**
Muslim **0.6%**

won't say **4%**

other or unspecified **2.5%**

non-religious **12.1%**

THE VATICAN
The Vatican is the center of the Christian Roman Catholic religion. Located in the center of Rome, Italy, it is the home of the Pope, who is the head of the Catholic church.

NIGERIA

Sacred sites
Scattered around the world are several places that are very important to the major religions. These sacred sites hold important buildings or venues to which millions of people travel on special journeys called **pilgrimages**.

NIGERIA

Christian **40%**

other or unspecified **10%**

Muslim **50%**

RELIGION

- Christian
- Muslim
- Non-religious
- Hindu
- Buddhist
- Jewish
- No clear majority

JERUSALEM, ISRAEL/WEST BANK
The city of Jerusalem is a sacred site for three major religions: Judaism, Christianity, and Islam.

AMRITSAR, INDIA
The Golden Temple, or Harmandir Sahib, at Amritsar in India is the center of the Sikh religion.

MECCA, SAUDI ARABIA
Every year, millions of Muslims make a pilgrimage, or Hajj, to Mecca, Saudi Arabia. Mecca is the birthplace of the prophet Muhammad and the holiest city in the religion of Islam.

VARANASI, INDIA
Located on the banks of the Ganges River, Varanasi is one of the most sacred sites in Hinduism. Millions of people come to the city to bathe in the river's holy waters.

SIZE OF RELIGIOUS GROUPS
% of the global population

Jewish **0.2%**
Other **6.7%**
Buddhist **7.1%**
Hindu **15%**
Unaffiliated **16.3%**
Muslim **23.2%**
Christian **31.5%**

BODH GAYA, INDIA
Said to be the spot where Gautama Buddha achieved enlightenment, Bodh Gaya is a sacred pilgrimage site to members of the Buddhist religion.

29

INDIA

INDONESIA

Muslim **87.2%**

INDONESIA

Hindu **1.7%**

Christian **9.8%**

other or unspecified **1.3%**

Hindu **80.5%**

INDIA

Muslim **13.4%**

Christian **2.3%**

Sikh **1.9%**

other or unspecified **1.9%**

—Mapping the—
WORLD

The maps in this book are two-dimensional representations of our sphere-shaped world. Maps allow us to display a huge range of information, including the size of the countries and where people live.

PROJECTIONS

Converting the three-dimensional world into a two-dimensional map can produce different views, called projections. These projections can show different areas of Earth.

GLOBE
Earth is shaped like a sphere, with landmasses wrapped around it.

CURVED
Some maps show parts of the world as they would appear on this sphere.

FLAT
Maps of the whole world show the landmasses laid out flat. The maps in this book use projections like this.

TYPES OF MAPS

Different types of maps can show different types of information. Physical maps show physical features, such as mountains and rivers, while political maps show countries and cities. Schematic maps show specific types of information, such as routes on a city subway network, and they may not necessarily show things in exactly the right place.

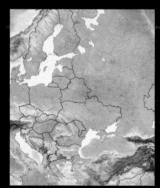

Physical map

Political map

Schematic map

MAP SYMBOLS

Maps use many symbols to show information, such as blue lines for rivers and dots for cities. Some of the symbols in this book show the locations of subjects, or the symbols are different sizes to represent different values—the bigger the symbol, the greater the value.

GLOSSARY

ANCESTOR
An individual or a species from which a modern person or species has descended, or come from

FAVELA
The Portuguese name given to the enormous shanty towns that grow in and around major cities throughout Brazil

GROSS DOMESTIC PRODUCT (GDP)
The value of the goods and services that are produced by a country over a year; the GDP can be shown as the total value produced by an entire country over a year, or as the average for each person living in that country (per capita)

HEALTH CARE
The people and facilities in a country that look after and protect a person's health, including clinics, hospitals, nurses, and doctors

LAND BRIDGE
A strip of land linking two large landmasses; during the last ice age, land bridges appeared linking North America to Asia and Australia to Asia. The land bridges allowed prehistoric humans and animals to migrate to these continents.

LIFE EXPECTANCY
The number of years a person can expect to live; life expectancy depends on a number of factors, including where a person lives, whether they are male or female, how long their parents lived, and their lifestyle

LITERACY
A person's ability to read and write

MAKESHIFT
Temporary and of low quality

MIGRATION
The movement of animals and humans from one region to another, usually in search of food, water, or a place to live and raise young

MONARCHY
A type of government in which the head of state is a king or queen

OBESITY
A medical condition in which a person has accumulated so much fat that it threatens his or her health

PILGRIMAGE
A journey made to a holy place

REPUBLIC
A type of government where the population votes in the people who will govern them

RESPIRATORY
Relating to your breathing system, including the lungs and airways

SANITATION
The safe disposal of waste, including human waste, and protecting people from coming into contact with that waste

URBANIZATION
The rate at which people move from the countryside into towns and cities

WARHEAD
The explosive part of a bomb or missile; warheads can be conventional or nuclear

31

WEBSITES

www.nationalgeographic.com/kids-world-atlas/maps.html
The map section of the National Geographic website where readers can create their own maps and study maps covering different topics.

www.mapsofworld.com/kids/
Website with a comprehensive collection of maps covering a wide range of themes that are aimed at students and available to download and print out.

www.cia.gov/library/publications/resources/the-world-factbook/
The information resource for the Central Intelligence Agency (CIA), this offers detailed facts and figures on a range of topics, such as population and transportation, about every single country in the world.

www.kids-world-travel-guide.com
Website with facts and travel tips about a host of countries from around the world.

INDEX